Ephemera Fair

Poems

of

darkness and light

By

Steve Douglas

Contents

Betjeman is spinning in his grave

Come, friendly words, fall on the page,
For poetry is quite the rage,
It doesn't matter what your age,
For Betjeman is spinning in his grave…

Come, rhymes and rhythms, tell your tale,
Don't be afraid to flop or fail,
Or worry as the Old Ones wail,
For Wordsworth is a-rumbling in the earth…

Come, metaphors, be armoured tanks,
Don't wait around for words of thanks,
Dismiss authorities and ranks,
For Ted Hughes must be seething in his cellar…

Come, free verse, explode with pride,
And spatter truth on every line,
Let no rule block your path of words
For Duffy has a place that's up for grabs…

Come, sweet words, complete the book,
So everyone will want to look,
Then let it simmer, let it cook,
For Betjeman is spinning in his grave.

Beware the wicked world

"Beware the Boogletosh when the moon's aglow,"
Said Mother Matilda to Little Joe.
"You'll hear him hobbling up the stairs –
"Leave the light on in case he's there."

"Avoid the Glubbs and the Doomwatch clan,
"Don't smile at the Swillbug," said gloomy Gran.
"Keep away from the Krusher," said Cousin Kate,
"Say your prayers to Jesus before it's too late!"

"Run when you hear the Rabberwing groan,"
Warned Uncle Bill and Aunty Joan.
"Go home when you meet the Glubbergrook,"
Boomed Big Brother Ben behind his book.

"These are the beasts of Halloween –
They're always there, but seldom seen!
The beasts are there," proclaimed Joe's Dad
"To punish you for when you're bad!"

And Little Joe trembled in his bed,
Their awful warnings in his head.
Of Terrors in the world out there,
With twisted teeth and tangled hair.

Of Rabberwings and Glubbs and such,
Who'd make him wither with their touch.
With wicked ways and cunning ploys
They'd gobble up both girls and boys.

But you and I and Little Joe
Should be extremely pleased to know -
The wicked world is not all bad,
But families can be quite quite mad…

Night beasts

I heard the hoot of a midnight owl
In the tangled trees outside.
Insects hissed through milky mist;
I crept away to hide.

I saw a spider still at work,
Her silken web was shining.
A beastly fly was caught inside -
She'll very soon be dining!

Across the floor with pit-a-pat
There scurried one brown mouse.
I set a trap should he come back,
But he had fled the house.

Around my light, around my light,
The mottled moth will flutter.
I have no doubt he'll not get out -
I've closed the wooden shutter.

And so to bed and hope and hope
The hungry bugs don't bite,
One greedy flea and I might be
Up scratching half the night.

The night is filled with presence,
Scratch and scrabblings in my home.
Night beasts are here, the morning's near,
Yet I shall wake alone.

A lighthouse keeper on Mars

At the centre stood the Goddess and I worshipped at her feet;
If I only tasted dust it was enough.
I would murder for her smile and be corrupted for her love;
If my soul were dark with cinders I would laugh!

But the centre has betrayed me and I stare into the void,
Where the stars have turned to darkness and to dust.
Where the ebbing of my life and mind has died a dismal death,
And the words that I can stutter are my last.

With the centre gone I move out to the edge of time and space,
Yet with no centre, edges cannot be.
Still I tempt the void to take me; I invite the blackness in,
I let all its darkest demons see the way.

The insinuating fingers of a beast that no one knows,
And all the world reduced to blood and bone:
As the void shows how alone I am, I stand and face the stars -
I can see no future with the centre gone.

There is only sullen silence and the dry and endless sand -
There is fire without warmth and without life.
Beyond my ancient outpost on the alien sea bed
There is random motion, chance and fate and chaos.

The centre is a god and he is worshipped by the stars,
But no people see his beauty or his truth.
If he stands alone, a lighthouse keeper stranded out on Mars,
Or Mankind upon the Earth it is enough.

Whenever we meet

Whenever we meet
The stars all change places
The moon peeps up over the hill.
The storm may crash down
On the stones on the beach
But around us is peaceful and still.

Whenever we laugh
The clouds lose their anger
The sky becomes cloudless and blue.
The sun warms the pebbles
That lie by the seashore,
Listening to me and to you.

Whenever we dream
The hills turn to valleys
The worn out and old become new.
The trees turn to rivers
The leaves fly like starlings
And anything can become true.

Whenever we part
The sun sinks in silence
The waves tease and torment the shore.
But the moon is still glowing
The pebbles all trembling
And waiting till we meet once more

Long ago

Once I heard the lilies singing,
Once I watched the wheat fields grow,
In my heart the summer ringing,
That was long ago.
Once I saw the green fields glisten,
Blades would quiver, breezes blow,
Once I'd watch and once I'd listen,
That was long ago.
Once I loved a dark haired lady,
Where she went I'd always go,
Once I felt there'd be no other,
That was long ago.
Once upon a time a dream
Inside my head would help me so,
Dreams are not enough to save me,
That was long ago.

Did I look for Nature's glory?
Fields of green or deepening snow?
Life was TV, books and records,
In the suburbs long ago.
Did I travel? Did I wander?
Making love where moonbeams glow?
Only in imagination,
In the suburbs long ago.
Would I go to my dark lady,
If I could undo time's flow?
Dancing back through all the decades
To the suburbs long ago?
In a room I dreamed a future,
Dreams were all I had to show,
Dreams alone no longer please me,
That was long ago.

An alternate life

She often wakes at 3am,
Always hot, her legs tangled in the sheets,
Always with glistening beads between her fallen breasts,
Her groin tingling with memories and longings…

Not for the husband who gave her a child,
Nor for the one who gave her thrills and bruises
In equal measure,
Nor the rock who gave her,
Finally,
Security and a measure of contentment.

Nor even for her lovers,
The many men who offered illicit excitement,
Secret meetings, snatched moments,
The release of pent up desires,
Pleasures more powerful for their imminent discovery,
A flood of moments against floors, doors, walls, damp earth,
Crushing leaves in private copses,
Beneath trees and skies, in beds and bathtubs,
Tangled with the bodies of men
Who touched her heart only briefly.

Nor even for the one woman
Who gave her the sweetest ecstasy of all,
The discovery of soft lips, slow building passion,
And silky skin.
None of these.

She remembers the summer with the boy she never had,
Whose eyes were deep and blue as long forgotten seas,
Whose talk was of dreams.
His hand was sweaty and he made her heart tremble,
Stilling her tongue with confusion.
A hesitant hand that once brushed tentatively, hopefully
Against her breast,
Rested on her knee, her thigh,
Fingers fluttering like a lost bird beneath her summer dress,
Until she thrust them away in feigned outrage.

The memory casts a chill down the decades of her life.
A hand once entwined with hers
Drifted away and never waved goodbye.

She often wakes at 3am,
Always with her legs tangled in the sheets,
Always longing to go back,
To take the hesitant hand from fifty years before,
Lead it across smooth flesh now patterned with cellulite
To rest upon a firm belly.
Trembling,
She would press slim fingers beneath damp cotton
To the moist folds of yesteryear,
Gaze into the lost, forgotten seas of what might have been,
Rising into an alternate life,
A life where she never wakes at 3am.

Readers' wives

I'm tempted by the top shelf
With its show of Readers' Wives,
And contact schemes for those with dreams
Of spicing up their lives.

The middle shelf has fashion mags,
I know what I'll find there -
Boobs and bums and flattened tums,
No hint of pubic hair.

Pages filled with bras and thongs,
And covers there to trick us,
They don't reveal the stark appeal
Of housewives with no knickers.

Nymphs with nipples covered up,
Starlets who cause a stir -
Or Mrs. Brown from out of town?
I know who I'd prefer.

Not summer babes with airbrushed limbs
Or groins made smooth with wax,
But feast my eyes on the dimpled thighs
Of "Jill from Halifax"!

I don't want skinny models
Who have slimmed to zero size,
But women blessed with real breasts,
And bellies, legs and thighs.

I don't want bottled fake tan skins
Or girls lined up in rows
Not teens or queens or babes in jeans
But a woman, with no clothes.

A woman who won't waste her time
In Rackham's or in Next,
But looks as though she knows you know
She's happier having sex.

I’m tempted by the top shelf
But I leave those mags behind;
For turning on when there is no one
I only need my mind.

The reincarnation of Gildas

When the skies have darkened,
And Glastonbury is once more the Isle of Avalon
And the words of politicians lie like autumn leaves,
Trodden beneath the boots of the masses
On hunger marches across the continents,
When the ice has thawed and fish swim through open windows
And the spores of the twentieth century cling to clothes
Too ragged to keep out the screaming winds
That shriek through the empty palaces
Of kingdoms that are no more,

Then he shall rise,

Sharpen his scythe on the lies of the multitudes,
Sever the heads of the innocent poppies,
Trample the withering leaves into pulp,
Turn all the colours to grey uniformity,
Baked in the ground, awaiting his master.

His limbs are tireless, his feet unrelenting,
His shadow casts over the land and the seas.
None shall escape him and many will thank him
As his final answer will silence their screams.

Until then,
I can only despair at the heat
Rising around the babble of politicians,
At the falling of gold into the bottomless pit
Of bombers, bullets and betrayals,
At the shrieking of souls who want only the mud hut
Savaged by naked flames in the night,
At the shivering of children, bereft of all aid
As winter approaches with its pitiless tread,
At the clogged arteries of the land,
Suffocating under the choke of the doomed beast,
Belching out in its death throes,
Swallowing the fragile leaves and petals of spring.
I can only curse at stupidity and short sightedness,
Laziness and greed, selfishness and intolerance,

The submission of values to the all-conquering secular creed.

Yet through it all, that vein of shame, that bowed head,
The acknowledgment of weakness and impotence,
The whispers of guilt,
For I am defendant and prosecutor as well as witness,
Too terrified to stand alone in the dock as Humanity looks on
With accusing, hypocritical eyes,
Too weak to walk into the onrushing crowds,
Too fearful to take up a cross,
Too aware of my own complicity,
Pointing my finger like a sixteenth century witch,
Charged with nothing, the awesome crime of inaction,
Of looking to private concerns,
Turning away from the TV screens, the powerless, the beggars,
The marginalised and disenfranchised, the bullied and the beaten,
The ostracised and libelled, the statistics, the numbers,
The masses that breed only more of the masses,
The bodies and blood and the bones and the meat,
Battered together into the homogeneous *them*.

Seduced instead
By the soma of soap, the glamour of rock 'n' roll,
The emptiness of celebrity, the roar of the crowd,
Indiscriminate nakedness on the World Wide Web,
Hearts, minds and bodies exposed for the scrutiny of the prurient,
Music sacrificed at the altar of the ringtone,
The endless voting for mediocrity,
The modern curse of reality TV;
Wife swaps that stop at the bedroom door
And swingers that go beyond it,
The catalogue of the country's worst,
Raised to godlike status and beamed into homes;
The angry drivers, the gluttonous, the belligerent neighbours,
The rampant indiscipline of children, forever wanting, wanting,
And the spineless concessions of cowardly parents,
That raging insistence that responsibility lies elsewhere;
A chorus of not guilty pleas.

We are all watching Big Brother as Big Brother watches us:
A million grainy images huddle together helplessly

As the intoxicated beat out each other's brains
And the Government banker pours alcohol down addicted throats,
Smiling as the cash flows into his coffers –
More fuel for the crusade to liberate distant lands,
To bring the hallowed chalice of democracy,
The noble offering of the West.

I died as the Dark Ages swallowed my land;
I have woken to an era blacker than pitch,
When monstrous snakes have slithered over every spare mile,
When no one believes in devils, yet devils are all around,
When no one believes in innocence, so innocence must be tarnished,
Corrupted, savaged, torn apart for entertainment,
When God is an empty word in an empty church,
For His prisoners long ago broke free,
And do what thou wilt is the whole of the law,
Exposure the only sin.

Still,
When my bones have crumbled once more into dust
And I float again in that oblivion,
Surrounded by all the souls who have ever lived -
Unaware of his rising,
Of his sweep across the remnants of the world his master formed,
Bringing hushed silence to the lush fields
And the cities decaying under grey ash,
Turning the innocent and guilty alike

Into waves

Or particles

Of light,

I shall bow to the Nemesis of all lives.

Persil the Chihuahua

Persil the Chihuahua has charisma style and power -
He's a Big **BIG** dog (though that is only in his head).
He struts around the Vale with Katie at his tail,
Expecting all the dogs in town to go where he has led.

Persil and Katie chased each other on an open field where the dogs would play,
All their friends were full of fun until the Council looked their way.
They didn't like dogs; they didn't like Persil; they didn't like Katie having a lark.
They wanted the field to turn into tarmac, for people had cars they needed to park.

But Persil the Chihuahua was a dog who'd never cower
He fought against intruders and was never known to fail…
With Foxy, Tazz and Katie his influence was weighty –
He united all the many dogs that lived around the Vale,

For Persil the Chihuahua would quite easily devour
Any dog he ever saw put Katie under threat.
He got the dogs together however bad the weather
He told them all their field was safe, that they weren't beaten yet –

The bulldozers came but the drivers soon saw there'd be no car park built that day;
At every entrance, on every corner, a pack of dogs was barring their way.
Corgis and Spaniels and Golden Retrievers, Alsatians and Terriers joining the hunt
For all those who wanted to threaten their field – and you can guess who was in front…

It was Persil the Chihuahua – the Champion of the hour
He led the fight and very soon the Council's fate was sealed.
The fight became a rout, and the Council voted out
And Persil led the dogs in celebration round the field –

For Persil the Chihuahua, with charisma, style and power
Fought against the Council with his tail held high
On that field beneath the skies if you open up your eyes
You'll see the dogs from round the town and hear their cry –
He's such a BIG **BIG** dog!
(Even though that's in his head)

Fish rising

We are rivers and our fish swim upstream,
Slippery and elusive above the stones.
We are divers and fisher folk too; we swim and part the waters
Or cast our lines again and again.

My fish tempts me and promises to surface
Next time, next time; only keep casting,
While yours rises and falls, sometimes between your fingers,
Sometimes gone, until finally you catch her tail -

Ride on through the flood,
Ripples turning to waves,
A rush beyond the edge as you gasp for air.
I see him in your wake,
Cast one final time and hook him,
Reeling,

Now **yes**

Now,

Our fish rise together from the deep.

We are carried away to the clouds

And fall like rain into another river.

No

The hidden people are training themselves not to feel,
To sleep without dreaming,
To wake without knowing,
Subservient to the numbers,
Rising and falling to the ticking god,
Surrendering consciousness to the abyss.

The silent people are abandoning thought,
Retreating from sensation,
Evaporating into body rhythms,
Nerve endings severed
And lost.

Silent and hidden,
The tyrannical thrust of conformity
Hammers its desire:
To engulf the spirit
That screams the instinctive "no"

NO

NO

NO

Striking a protest
At the mechanised world.

The pebble that stood alone (for Syd)

I see you at the doorway to '66,
Guitar over your shoulder,
Eyes twinkling at the beckoning road to fame.

I see you at the exit of '67,
Withered flowers swallowed
In the darkness of eyes that gaze
On an acid vision of inner space,
Behind the barricaded door.

I hear your distant strumming through the pain of '69,
Your word gems polluted by slithers of stone,
Fragmenting,
Piercing eyes that have seen too much.

I read of your seclusion through the decades of darkness,
Your final return to the Earth,
To your garden,
Able still to look at the sky and the river
And find it good.

A sentinel for a forgotten world,
You closed the door on the Sixties -

The pebble that stood alone.

Sleeping underwater

I am sleeping underwater - not even fish disturb me;
No one notices my slumber on my deep and silent bed.
I thought that I was swimming and I thought that someone knew me,
But "you're sleeping underwater" were the words inside my head.

"Your eyes are closed up tightly and you cannot hear me calling -
"When I speak your name and call into the deep.
"And no matter if I want you and no matter if you need me,
"If your consciousness has drifted and your brain has gone to sleep."

When sleeping underwater you can't see the fishes staring,
Though five fathoms up is blue sky and the air.
There may be a tsunami when withdrawing waves reveal you,
But you're sleeping underwater - you don't care.

Someone sleeping underwater as he stirs his morning coffee,
As he rides the train and dreams that he is free.
Eyes are open, bubbles bursting from the lips that are not speaking,
He would swim up to the surface if he knew it was the sea.

As he sleeps his lungs are filling even as he drinks his coffee,
No more breathing, no more thinking and the journey's end's in sight.
We are sleeping underwater as we smile and say "good morning",
Will we wake up and start living? Will we wake before the night?

The pixies of Pixintone

On Midsummer Eve,
Or so I believe,
The pixies of Pixintone dance through the woods.
They become very bold,
Or so I've been told,
And they lose all their fears and they cast off their hoods.

Their bodies are bright
With a violet light,
And their wings flutter softly to carry them by.
Their voices sing out
As they all dance about
But the sound is no more than a whispering sigh.

This magical sound,
Or so I have found
Drifts across to the cities that lie far away.
Though faint as light breathing,
This sound we're receiving -
It whispers and murmurs around us each day.

Midsummer Eve brings
All the light from their wings
And it sparkles around us and lasts for a year.
Though Pixintone lies
Neath the strangest of skies,
We could all feel its power pulsating round here.

Each year it gets stronger -
They dance a while longer,
And closer and closer towards us they come.
They'll do all they can
To bring magic to Man -
It will be all around when the pixies have done.

Now if you believe
And you feel a strong need
To escape from your world in your own special way,
If you hear a strange sound

And see lights all around -
It's the pixies of Pixintone coming your way!

Archimedes Twiddly

My 99 lovers

The first was dark,
The second fair,
The third was you.

The other 96 were imaginary.

Tattoo

You show me your tattoo
Hoist up your skirt
Inch by inch
Unselfconsciously revealing
Pale   freckled   legs

My gaze falls on your calves
Climbs high enough for only
Close   intimate   eyes

You show me your tattoo
I stroke its contours
Praise the design
My hand brushes your briefs
Soft   white   cotton

I'm teased by beckoning curls
Escaping like question marks
Sly   golden   hair

You show me your tattoo
I admire your courage
Openness to pain
Praise your resilience to
Ink   stinging   needles

You mock my hypocrisy
Press my hand to your heat
Burning   eager   pleasure

I never speak of your tattoo again.

Beauty

She totters on high heels,
Weaving and giggling through the Saturday night crowd,
Bare legs stricken by the winter air,
Face designed to please,
Hair dyed in fashionable tints.
But her soul peeps through at the roots;
A dark mystery.
Wipe the mask from her face and cover her gooseflesh,
Seat her at a quiet table with a book,
Free the dark mystery
And she would be beautiful.

Books

A million voices call out from oblivion,
Their dusty, croaking sounds muffled by time.
Happy to find rest in a dark corner
Of a dark attic,
Nestling snugly together in prose and rhyme,
The words of worlds hold hands and dance,
Nation with Nation.

Where books burn there is shrieking amidst the flames,
Their blackened pages the most bitter mortality.

In libraries of the future absurdity embraces wisdom,
And tolerance bigotry,
While Literature smiles upon the diaries of the masses.

All share holiness in the shelter of the book.

Dark figure running

Newsreel repeats:
Balloon burning
Filling the skies.
Beneath -
Dark figure running.
Newsman cries.

Engulfed
By fear,
By fiery breath;
Dark figure running.
Motionless in death.

We are the dark figure running,
However great our gains.
Above,
The Hindenburg,
Falling in flames.

Cocktails at eight

It's cocktails at eight, and I mustn't be late,
And I mustn't say anything dumb.
I stare at the floor as I knock at the door,
Then I'm in and the party's begun.

My hostess greets me graciously and points me at the wine,
She smiles, but no doubt curses my arriving right on time;
When coats get piled upon the bed, the bottom one is mine!

It's cocktails at eight, a more terrible fate
I couldn't think up if I tried.
I could have stayed home, but I'm here all alone,
And my stomach is churning inside.

The guests are all arriving, but there's no-one that I know,
I hold my drink, I nod and smile, politely say "hello".
I'll stand and listen to their tales until it's time to go.

It's cocktails at eight and I cannot relate
To this evening of meaningless chat.
The girls stand with glasses; the boys all make passes -
Don't fancy my chances at that!

For over in the corner stands the man with all the charm,
Seductive smile and so of course a girl upon each arm,
Both listening attentively to some long winded yarn.

It's cocktails at nine and this glass isn't mine -
Someone else must be drinking my coke.
I could almost walk out, for there isn't much doubt -
I have nothing to say to these folk.

I'm surrounded by accountants talking figures in my head,
I think about my boring job and feel my face turn red,
Announce that I'm a writer and the conversation's dead.

It's cocktails at nine; it's a wonderful time
For an outgoing, extrovert guy.
I have to agree, but it isn't for me,

For I'm not and I cannot think why.

I can hear quite ridiculous laughter, as Charmer is telling his jokes,
The girls think he's dashing and super - incredibly sexy (he hopes!),
So I dash off upstairs to the bedroom and rummage around in the coats.

It was cocktails at ten; I was wondering when
All the chatter would finally stop.
I'd been standing all night - not a chair was in sight;
I was just about ready to drop.

Now it's cocktails at one - it's three hours I've been gone,
Walking all the way home in the rain.
And "wherever is Steve?" someone asks, "did he leave?"
Someone says, "no - I don't think he came."

Almost the end

He moved so slowly,
The old man.
Step by painful step,
He passed us as we sat,
Ready to end it.
And we watched.

The guilt hung in the air -
We should not be there.
The old man moved,
We sat,
Eternity waited.

They fell so silently,
Your tears.
A trickle on cold cheeks.
Our beating hearts, our moving minds,
Eyes following old legs,
Obliterated any time now.

We carried on.

Coffee shop

She sips her cappuccino and leafs through the paper
Abstractedly.

Is she passing the hours as the drizzle runs down the window?
Or waiting for the boyfriend who is always late?

Does she tuck into the chocolate fudge?
Or shy away, remembering her figure?

Are the creases by her eyes the results of last night's party?
Or the years that have passed her by?

Is she alone and ready to flirt with passing strangers?
Or lonely and talking to anyone who will listen?

She sips her cappuccino and gazes into the street.
Is she sixteen or sixty?

And does it matter?

Ode to a feminist

A feminist will approach you first and ask you for a date,
She'll share the cost of any trip (though sometimes she'll be late).
A feminist won't mind putting petrol in the car,
And share the driving when you're travelling far.

A feminist out hiking takes the rucksack half the time,
And when you go off on your own won't stay at home and pine.
A feminist will never shelter underneath your wing,
But go out with her friends and never cling.

A feminist will approach the bar and buy a round of drinks,
If you ask for her opinion, she'll tell you what she thinks.
A feminist will take you out and treat you to a meal,
Encourage you to tell her how you feel.

A feminist won't expect you to be good at DIY,
And when she watches sentimental films will never cry.
So treasure every minute that you have to share the chores
And never ever say that she is yours!

Should you be trying to find a girl exactly like your Mum,
But come across a feminist, and think you ought to run -
Be liberated, change your ways, and one day you'll be glad,
For she'll never want a boy like dear old Dad!

Delayed

Suppose we find a body,
Drifting,
Face down among the ducks,
Where no body ought to be?

We'd have to haul it out,
Reaching helplessly,
Tugging at bloated flesh.

And then?
Brought to the bank,
Staring at unrecognisable features,
Wondering who she was and why she was floating there.

The nearest phone a mile away, but no hurry;
She's dead, after all, though her family still wonder.
The call made, we'd wait anxiously for reinforcements.

Ambulance.
Police. There will be questions,
Though we know nothing, only went for a stroll
Along the canal bank,
Killing time before we leave.

The sun shines, but a sunnier day awaits us
If we catch our flight,
So perhaps no stroll by the canal tonight;
Suppose we find a body?

The death of technology

With apology to Prometheus
I pilot a neon dream
In a crackle of paper feather,
Grimace at the techno nightmare,
Angle a rumour of love into the light
And soar above the poison in the seas.
I return fire to the gods
Hoping for the generous blessings of a tired Earth.

Migraine

The Beast is awake!
He sits malevolently on my skull,
Tendrils tightening around my forehead,
Breathes his threats into my ear:
"I am coming!"
I launch an attack, but nothing,
No drug coursing through my bloodstream
Halts his progress.

The Beast is here!
He spears a jagged spike above my eye,
Twisting and boring into my brain.
"Your day is mine!"
The harsh white of paper dazzles,
Trembling fingers, sweating palms
Tell of his presence.

The Beast is inside!
He seals my gut and stirs the poison round,
Swirls the muck in time to distant thunder.
"Taste my victory!"
The unstoppable rise of undigested lunch
Spatters itself around the bucket.

The Beast is triumphant!
He's battered my brain, choked me with vomit,
Thrown me to the mercy of the darkened room,
Turned my curses to pleas, my defences shattered.
I rise and pace and sprawl and twist,
To loosen his vice, finally relenting,
Bowing in shame before his feet.
Sated, he lets the darkness flood in,
Leaving only that dull, distant, pulsing reminder
Behind my eyes.
And in my ears his promise:
"I will come again."

Searching for the Boblebone

I tried to find the Boblebone,
I searched and searched again.
I looked outside, I looked at home,
I asked my Uncle Ben.

He called a spade a spade
And said "you're worse than Cousin Bob!
Get out and learn a trade,"
He said. "Get out and find a job!"

I found a job inside a week,
But that became a bore.
Before too long I had to seek
The Boblebone once more.

My mates said "Bill, it don't exist!
Come out and let's get drunk!"
So down the pub, we all played whist,
But all my hopes had sunk.

I met a lass called Sally, who
Was standing near my gate.
She showed me things that we could do -
The Boblebone could wait!

We did it once, we did it twice -
Went walking in the rain.
The first time it was rather nice,
The second, not the same.

So Sally left, and Jean, and Joan,
And Jill and Jan and Glad -
When I talked about the Boblebone,
They thought that I was mad!

I sauntered here, I wandered there,
I travelled far and wide,
Always seeking places where
The Boblebone might hide.

I was used to being on my own
When I encountered you.
I still looked for the Boblebone,
But fancy - you did too!

We curled up warm and snug in bed,
You reached and pulled me near.
I kissed your lips, you smiled and said
"The Boblebone is here."

A family of Haiku

1

Confetti cascade
Bride carried over threshold
Curtains closed all day

Midwife's cheery smile
Mother cradles new daughter
Pink ribbon flutters

Father drowns in ale
Holy water scooped from font
Congregation increasing

3am baby
Banshee bawls for attention
One more sleepless night

Baking day at home
Mother's sticky jam fingers
Father burns his tongue

Father's hippo yawn
Bluebottle loses his way
Teatime comes early

2

Aunt Maud comes for tea
Pennies pressed in tiny hands
Jolly smiles all round

Cousin Harry grins
Bullies when Mum looks away
Swift kick stops his smile

Football in Gran's yard
Seven-year-old Rooney shoots
New window needed

Grandma loses teeth
Bares gums at watching pussy
Cat's smug Cheshire smile

Modern family
Mum and Dad work long and late
Play station king reigns

Newlyweds next door
Passionate cries through the wall
Nostalgia beckons

3

Bed creaks at midnight
Kids camp under starry skies
Mum and Dad's playtime

Boyfriend's fingers stray
Knickers lost under sofa
Chemist visit soon

Daughter parades ring
Father practices his speech
Confetti cascade

Loss

The dinner plate stands erect and lonely
On the drainer.
A single soap bubble clings to its edge,
Illuminated by a sunbeam from the chill March morning,
Dancing on the flowery pattern,
The design she loved and I thought twee.
Below, in the drawer,
Its mate lies unused,
The dust on its surface marking the days
She has been gone.

The soil came from beneath the rose tree she tended,
Scattered like pebbles on the coffin lid,
Coughing like an old man.
Roses rise like sympathetic soldiers each summer.
I do not see them; it is the soil I envy,
For only the soil went with her to eternity.

Death

Death is a coward.
He only visits those too weak to resist.

Death is lonely
And lacking social graces;
He visits once
And is never asked back.

He shrieks with envy of our memories,
Our capacity for love,
Our versatility and courage,
Our disregard of him.
He is a gnat on the immensity of the Universe,
Seething with impotent fury
At any indifferent back,
Greedy for life and attention.

Lady Death?
Of course Death is male:
He does only one thing, after all.

Ephemera fair

I wander the ephemera fair,
Stop and scrabble, rummage, stare.
Scraps once loved by multitudes,
Now only old collectors care.

Postcards of forgotten places,
Photographs of unknown faces,
All the flotsam time erases,
Saved at the ephemera fair.

Politicians of all nations,
Books of self-justifications,
Newspapers with brown-edged covers,
Ration books like wartime lovers,
Book sets banded up like brothers,
Only normal wear and tear.

Faces from forgotten times,
Like dusty books of ancient rhymes,
Junk and love swept by the ages,
Leaving only speckled pages.
Treasure sought is never there,
I cannot find it anywhere.

Lost in the ephemera fair,
I think I glimpse your auburn hair,
For seconds then your gaze is caught,
The hazel eyes, the smile I sought.
I look again; you are not there,
No more at the ephemera fair.

A sleepwalker, I step outside,
Dropped cruelly where nostalgia hides.
See people rush like rising tides,
No pause, reflection, doubt or care.
A breeze blows sadness through my hair
I watch the moment passing there -
The world as an ephemera fair.

Lovemaking

Love is not the flower
Love is not the painting
Love is not the symphony

Love is the attention
Of the gardener
The artist
The composer

Only in love can beauty be created
Only in beauty can love be made

Blocked

How can I not write?

Blank screen taunts my sterile fingers,
Numb and dry and silent still.
Paper pale with death and sickness,
Numbers dancing down to nil.

Ink is stilled like blood in bodies
Dead decaying into dust.
Sentenced to a time of silence -
How can I not write? I must.

In ten thousand cells the white walls
Taunt the lovers of the word.
Isolation, deprivation
Will not stop them being heard.

How can I not write?

Never change

They never change.

They speak the words of yesterday,
Words dancing into worlds.
Frodo still slips on the ring,
Smeagol slyly betrays.
Black clawed letters sneer
Or smile,
But never change.

Diamond point tracks the grooves of yesterday,
Soundwave through time.
The Star Spangled Banner electrifies a continent,
The Fab Four scream "yeah! yeah!" through the years
But never change.

Flat figures dance on the screen into yesterday.
A black and white Bogie is looking at you kid,
And Marilyn never died,
The smile that still cries 'save me'
Will never change.

We never change,
Compassion and cruelty of a million yesterdays.
Inquisitors eradicate tolerance,
Chasing the centuries for the mark of the witch.
And serial murder
Stars
In the modern amphitheatre;
Caligula claps: a million TV sets hum.
Thumbs down for change.

Essence

I was thinking about John Lennon,
How he very nearly won,
In my thoughts were starting over,
The voice, the song, the gun…

I was thinking about that epigram:
"Whom the gods notice, they destroy,"
How triumph has its bitter taste,
How sadness crushes joy.

I thought of Wilfred Owen,
And the battle on the Somme,
His survival in the trenches,
How when peace came he was gone.

And the world – its deepest essence,
Antagonistic to us all;
When we raise our fists in triumph
It determines we must fall.

I was thinking about John Lennon,
How he was slipping free,
How the world dismantles freedom,
How its essence could find me…

Creedlycrest for tea

Creedly-crests leave creedly traces
Creeping from cracks and creedly places,
I'm going to wipe all the smirks from their faces
And once at the end of some creedly chases
Have creedly-crest for tea!

> Whoever are we? Whoever are we?
> The creedly-crests and me?
> They go with a slither all hither and thither
> They'll cover the Earth if they get any bigger.
> They're in for a shock when they meet up with me,
> Cause it's creedly-crest for tea!

Over the rush of the salty sea,
Inside of a log that they cut from a tree,
Our tummies a-heaving so vi-o-lent-lee,
The creedly-crests and me.

Up to the sinister side of the moon,
We flew and we blew in a yellow balloon,
All singing and humming a creedly tune,
The creedly-crests and me.

> Whoever are we? Whoever are we?
> The creedly-crests and me?
> They go with a slither all hither and thither,
> They'll cover the Earth if they get any bigger,
> So I'm going to track 'em and watch 'em all wither,
> Cause I have the feelin' that they are appealin' -
> I'll oil 'em and boil 'em and try not to spoil 'em,
> Confess, you can guess what they'll be -
> They'll be creedly-crest for tea, you'll see,
> I'll have creedly-crest for tea.

So far, so far away they flee,
So far, so far away from me,
Their tummies a-fluttering so trem-u-lous-lee,
Cause it's creedly-crest for tea.

Now down they went in a creedly crack,
They dug and they dug, but they never came back,
Cause I was there with 'em and fancied a snack -
My creedly-crest for tea!

> Whoever were we? Whoever were we?
> The creedly-crests and me?
> They were really quite grimy, and creepy, and slimy,
> The stars of this verse that's so rhythm 'n' rhymey,
> And I must report that they tasted sublimey
> And knew in the end they were destined to be
> My creedly-crest for tea!

It was worth the rush of the salty sea,
And the ride to the moon where we flew so free,
But a crack in the Earth is the place to be,
Having creedly-crest for tea,
Just me,
Having creedly-crest for tea.

(Archimedes Twiddly)

Uncarved

A new day sits like a block of rosewood,
Untouched,
Uncarved.
Make of it what you will.
Create with it, then let go.

Time is a string of coloured beads,
Each moment disappears into the past,
As you reach for the next,
Untouched,
Uncarved.

Frost

He leaves magical messages etched on the window,
Taunting with a brilliance born of ice,
Gleefully sealing us in a cold cruel capsule,
Dipping spiky hands in the heating.

A crystal shroud cloaks the lawn,
A landscape in monochrome, sharply
Throwing back his icicle fingers;
He stabs bitter patterns in a crescendo of creation.

Dreams freeze on every surface,
Triumphant sheets of silver await the sun -
His tragic lover.
He embraces destruction for a moment of beauty.

On childhood's track

I couldn't deal with feelings,
Nor any outward show.
No, no, never where people could see.
You came as an early spring,
Feeling for me.

We lay together in the park,
The summer long and hot.
I showed you everything I was,
And all that I was not...

October beckoned with bare branches;
You followed. I remained,
In the blissful innocence of June,
When the elves still danced among the flowers.

I stood on childhood's track.
I could have called you back.
I would have,
But I couldn't deal with feelings.

It all began with the Gingatot

My car is like a foreign zone,
With language that is all its own.
I don't know any of the parts;
I don't care - if it stops and starts,
So when one day the monster broke
I had to see the garage bloke.

He said "it's plain to see you've got
An old and worn out gingatot."
"The gingatot?" I said. "All right -
I'll bring it in tomorrow night."
"A simple job, say twenty quid,"
He said, and quickly closed the lid.

I nod and smile as if to say
"I know about such things, okay?"
But all I ask is my car runs -
The bits inside are umblybums.
Now twenty quid is not a lot
To replace a worn out gingatot.

Next night the man had more to say:
"Been working on that car all day -
The gingatot has snapped the cog -
The rogitator will not jog.
The binsack cord has too much play,
So could you leave it one more day?"

Two days later, back I trek,
To find the thing's not mended yet.
"The rampack has completely gone -
I've had to fit another one!
The back end gospot's leaking too,
But I've fixed all of that for you."

"I've had to change the sparrowjack,
(The leaking gospot ruined that!)
And so, of course, the slug gun's stuck -
The sock head's got all full of muck.
It's bent the left hand burjit seal
And misaligned the steering wheel."

I saw the bank, took out a loan,
And drove my mended car back home.
"It's all right now," the garage said,
But my account was in the red,
And so I'm broke - I just can't win;
I can't afford to put petrol in.

So, if you're searching near and far
To find another motor car,
Check every single umblybum,
Or you may find your car won't run,
Because you foolishly forgot
To note the state of the gingatot...

Psychopath

Holy and unholy lands entwined,
Discoloured light delights the darkened mind,
While from without the raging figures spin,
And doubtful vigour snares the world within.

Holy and unholy thoughts enmeshed;
Reality by fantasies caressed,
While in the distance silver light is spied
By dark deceptions dwelling deep inside.

Holy and unholy actions burst
From wild and twisted torments cruelly cursed;
An innocent terror filled with hate unfurled
At unsuspecting innocents in an unsuspecting world.

Golden dawn

In travelling through regions cold,
Where flowers fade and love is cast
Into the darkness of the past,
Where dwells the heart of one so bold,
And dreams survive and faith grows old,
I came upon you and was born,
The sun that brings the golden dawn.

While lost within the darkest night
Where spectres dance and demons screech
And angels stand beyond my reach,
Where devils too distort my sight
And dark clouds flood the inner light,
I found in you a chance to live,
The sun that light to Earth shall give.

While stranded in my darkest hour
When fearful thoughts pervade the air
Infringing on my bleak despair,
Like blooms upon a wilting flower,
My hopes and joys by fear devoured,
I came on you and rose above,
To find through all I still could love.

Moonlight swimming

Monday mornings claw me down
And shred my royal velvet gown
They burn my brain and crack my crown
In midnight moonlight swimming

Sundays shine and Mondays weep
For the tick-tock taps on the bridge of sleep
Towards the dawn its fingers creep
To stop my moonlight swimming

Monday sings a funeral tune
Throws Winter light inside my room
And shaken from the fading moon
I long for moonlight swimming

Monday wears her cruellest frown
And tears my feathered eiderdown
She sucks me through a market town
No longer moonlight swimming

Monday is a mournful day
She drains my colour, turns me grey
But cannot stop my flight away
To midnight moonlight swimming

The nothing box

Neighbours closed curtains
Shuttered eyes
Not seeing the black beetle
And the nothing box

He sat in silence
Words meant to comfort were
Puny
A sandcastle against a tsunami

Friends back through the years
Tenuous correspondences
Telephone conversations, e-mails, Christmas cards
Distant hellos: close goodbyes

Through silence he shouts
Go back to your lives
To your homes, to laughter
Throw back the shutters and allow in the sunshine

He would swap the crowded church
Sympathetic smiles
For the one
In the nothing box

The Artist

Eva Zargetti is naked today
There in the Gallery. Admission is free.
Eva Zargetti has something to say -
Important to strive: better to be.

Eva Zargetti owns language's power,
There on the page. Her words will play,
Shy. Trembling. Behind words she could cower,
But Eva Zargetti is naked today.

Eva Zargetti has nowhere to hide;
No novel, no poem, no artist's display.
Her body is open revealing her pride,
For Eva Zargetti is naked today.

Eva has public who study her skin,
Her breasts and her belly. Her dark pubic hair
Missing the essence, the Eva within
And Eva Zargetti is ceasing to care.

Eva Zargetti is going away,
Her message is lost. Her cry is unheard.
But Eva Zargetti is naked today,
Tomorrow once more she will hide behind words.

Travel

The gods are within
And the gods are infinite

What need then of travel?

When the mind is still
And the gods awaken
Everywhere is

Here

And

Now

An old Bob Dylan song

The postcard seller stopped me, and said I looked depressed.
She said "I thought you different but you're just like all the rest!"
She didn't even know me, so I guess I was impressed,
Because it's true, I'm feeling blue; I'm lonely, tired and stressed.
In all the cities of the world there's no place I belong,
Yes, here am I, stuck deep inside an old Bob Dylan song.

The carnival had come to town to sell me coloured dreams,
I saw the fortune teller, who said "nothing's as it seems."
I looked at all her cards and thought "I wonder what she means."
While outside by the calliope I heard the fat man's screams.
But when the midget winked at me I thought "there's something wrong."
For it's no lie, I'm stuck inside an old Bob Dylan song.

The hangman was approaching and I thought I saw him smile,
I turned away, escaped inside a love affair a while,
But he kept right on coming for me mile on dusty mile.
I thought he'd try to trick me but that's really not his style,
And he thinks I'm weak and helpless but I'm really very strong -
No need to hide when you're stuck inside an old Bob Dylan song.

The girl I loved was smiling; you could tell that she was pleased
That after all these lonely years she'd got me on my knees,
I would have loved her even then however much she teased,
Take my advice and don't think twice 'bout any new disease,
However many pretty girls you find yourselves among,
Love one who's tried, who's stuck inside an old Bob Dylan song.

I thought my life was over, I was thinking of the past,
The good times had all been and gone; I knew they wouldn't last,
I held the blade against my wrist; I thought the die was cast,
I knew then that a single stroke would end my life and fast
But then I heard a voice that said "be silent; still your tongue -
"You not alive, you're stuck inside an old Bob Dylan song."

I held my head, I looked above at grey and darkening skies
As all the many characters saw right through my disguise.
And where I'd looked for truth I found that everything was lies
They all said "don't you worry, man, 'cause you're becoming wise
Remember that and you'll find it's not hard to get along -
No need to cry when you're stuck inside an old Bob Dylan song."

The times they were a changing and the record was a turning
Beyond the gates of Eden there was nothing to be learning,
And like a rolling stone I moved, with all my senses churning
I left them all on Desolation Row, my bridges burning.
The song is over now and I can tell I don't belong,
For why should I be stuck inside an old Bob Dylan song?

Enough

Your summer smile
was enough

to scoop the coldness from me,
shatter the icicle bars,
flood red shame over my face,
pour honey over the pain.

More than enough.

I remember you
in autumn.

I remember living
in the space behind your eyes,
a crystal in the stained glass of your mind.

I remember dying
in the clenched cracks of your fingers,
broken clay cast into nothingness.

Winter betrayal,
a black hole.

It swallows all nobility,
crushes adulation,
compresses all love
into a bitter stone of fury.

Spring awakens memories.
I take the fury,
mock its power,
viciously carve it
into an image of your smile.

Enough.

Sunrise

The sunrise of all beginnings
Is first a shimmer,
A glow upon the dark horizon.
Light spreads across the sky,
The illusion of a flaming orb
Is complete.

The Earth turns steadily in silent contentment,
A new beginning flooding its surface
Somewhere,
In an eternal sunrise
Of now.

Still

Canopy of green
Above my outstretched body
Beneath, the Earth turns.

Other titles available

Confessions of a piano-pusher – growing up in the 60s: a childhood memoir covering my life from 1955 to 1969

Fernando the Storyteller: strange tales – a collection of short stories

Messages in Silver: a compilation of short stories, poetry and some extracts from Confessions.

Coming soon – The lost village of Shannon-by-the-sea: a fantasy novel.

'No' first appeared in The Ugly Tree
'The pebble that stood alone' first appeared in Zabadak
'Night beasts' first appeared in Telling Tales anthology

Thanks to Janet Hughes for 'Betjeman'
Thanks to Brian Wood for inspiring 'Gingatot'
Thanks to **Archimedes Twiddly** for 'The Pixies of Pixintone' and 'Creedlycrest for tea.'

www.ingramcontent.com/pod-product-compliance
Ingram Content Group UK Ltd.
Pitfield, Milton Keynes, MK11 3LW, UK
UKHW012254240726
13966UKWH00004B/1415